What Do You Know About
Colonial America

PowerKiDS press
New York

Lynn George

Published in 2008 by The Rosen Publishing Group, Inc.
29 East 21st Street, New York, NY 10010

First Edition

Editor: Joanne Randolph
Book Design: Kate Laczynski
Photo Researcher: Nicole Pristash

Photo Credits: Cover, pp. 1, 7, 8, 10, 11, 12, 13, 14, 15, 16, 17, 18 (bottom), 19, 20, 21 © Getty Images; p. 18 (top) Courtesy of the Library of Congress Geography and Map Division.

Library of Congress Cataloging-in-Publication Data

George, Lynn.
   What do you know about colonial America? / Lynn George. — 1st ed.
      p. cm. — (20 questions: history)
   Includes bibliographical references and index.
   ISBN 978-1-4042-4185-5 (library binding)
   1. United States—History—Colonial period, ca. 1600–1775—Miscellanea—Juvenile literature. 2. Children's questions and answers. I. Title.
   E188.G377 2008
   973.2—dc22
                                        2007031102

Manufactured in the United States of America

Contents

Colonial America

Before the United States was a country, it was a small group of **colonies**. People came to these colonies from Europe. They left behind the Old World they knew and came to what they called the New World. They found the New World strange. The Native Americans had a different way of life from theirs. The plants and animals were different, too.

Who were these **colonists**? Why did they come? When did they come? Where did they build settlements? What was life like for them? How did they get along with Native Americans? If you wonder about these things, keep reading.

The Old World included places like Britain, Spain, and Portugal in Europe. The New World was made up of North America and South America.

North America

Europe

Asia

Africa

South America

Australia

1. Why are we going to this strange place?

Many colonists went to the New World to find a better life. Many others went so they could practice their **religion** freely. Still others went to escape war.

2. When does the ship leave?

The English first attempted to found a colony in 1585. It was on Roanoke Island, near the coast of North Carolina. They deserted it in 1586. They founded their first lasting settlement, at Jamestown, Virginia, in 1607. Many more colonists came during the next 150 years. They founded settlements along North America's eastern coast.

Here the first settlers land at Jamestown in 1607.

This map shows the British colonies and territories on the East Coast of America.

3. Who is that in the seat next to me?

Most of the colonists were English. Some were French, German, Dutch, Scottish, or Irish. Some colonists were rich. Others were poor.

7

4. Are you sure this is the right place?

Colonists discovered that life was hard in the strange, new land. They had to cut down trees before they could build houses and plant crops. Sometimes the land was not good for farming. Sometimes there was no good drinking water. Winter weather could be terrible. To top it off, Native Americans did not always welcome their new neighbors.

Native Americans attacked Jamestown in 1608.

In 1587, the English tried again to settle Roanoke Island. The first English baby born in America was born there. She was named Virginia Dare. When a supply ship arrived in 1590, everyone was gone. Nobody is sure what happened to the Lost Colony.

Virginia Dare was baptized in 1587 on Roanoke Island. She was the granddaughter of the settlement's governor, John White.

6. Where is the gold?

More than 100 colonists founded Jamestown in 1607. They were interested mostly in finding gold. The settlement had problems right away. The land was bad for crops. The water was bad. Many people died from sickness and lack of food. Algonquian Native Americans killed others. Then John Smith became the colony's leader. He saved the colony by making people work hard.

Jamestown was on the coast between the Atlantic Ocean and the James River. Here the colony is shown in 1615.

Here Pocahontas kneels next to John Smith. She raises her hand to keep the Native American warrior from killing him.

7. Did Pocahontas really save John Smith?

Algonquians caught John Smith. Smith was later told that they were going to kill him. A young princess named Pocahontas is said to have saved him. More likely, what really happened was that Smith was made part of the tribe during a special service.

John Smith was born in 1580 and left home when he was 16. He had many adventures before sailing for the New World in December 1606.

8. I forget. Am I a Pilgrim or a Puritan?

A mixed group of people founded Plymouth Colony in 1620. Some were Puritans. Some were part of a group called Separatists. Others came looking for riches. They had no special name for themselves. However, people in later times called all of them Pilgrims. We still call them that today.

9. Are we there yet?

The Pilgrims traveled for two months on a crowded ship called the *Mayflower*. They ate mostly cold meat or fish and bread. Much of the food went bad before they reached America.

The Mayflower Compact was signed in November 1620.

After the *Mayflower* arrived, 41 men signed the Mayflower **Compact**. They promised to make fair laws for the good of everyone.

The Pilgrims landed at Plymouth, Massachusetts, on December 11, 1620.

11. Are you sure this is how to grow this?

The first year at Plymouth Colony was hard. Sickness and lack of food killed about half the colonists. In spring 1621, some Wampanoag Native Americans came to meet the colonists. A man named Tisquantum stayed with the colonists. They called him Squanto. He taught them how to grow corn, pumpkin, and beans. He showed them where to fish, too.

The settlers had to make many of their own goods. This man is making bricks that will be used to build things like chimneys.

The colonists at Plymouth feasted after their first **harvest** in fall 1621. They invited their Wampanoag neighbors. Today this is often called the first Thanksgiving. The colonists and Wampanoags ate ducks, geese, eels, pumpkin, corn, beans, carrots, **turnips**, spinach, and maybe dried blueberries.

The colonists shared their first harvest with their Native American neighbors.

13. Can we all just get along?

Native Americans and colonists had different ways of life. Most colonists believed in one God. Native Americans believed in many spirits. They also believed that all living things were joined.

Colonists believed that one person could own land. Native Americans believed that land belonged to the tribe.

Colonies had rich and poor people. Women and people without land had little power. Members of Indian groups were more equal. Women had power.

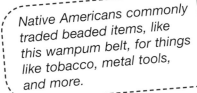

Native Americans commonly traded beaded items, like this wampum belt, for things like tobacco, metal tools, and more.

Here colonists and Native Americans are trading at Jamestown.

At first, many Native Americans helped colonists. The differences caused problems, though. Indians fought to make the colonists leave. The colonists fought back. They were not planning on going anywhere.

14. Do you think 13 is an unlucky number?

By 1733, the English had 13 colonies. The first colony, in Virginia, was started in 1607. Next was Massachusetts in 1620. Then came New Hampshire, New York, Connecticut, Maryland, Rhode Island, Delaware, Pennsylvania, North Carolina, New Jersey, South Carolina, and Georgia.

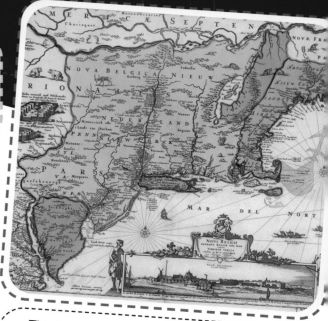

This is a map of New Netherland, which was formed by the Dutch.

Peter Stuyvesant was the leader of the Dutch colony of New Netherland. He was a strict leader, who worked hard to keep order in the colony.

15. Were there other colonies?

Other European countries also had colonies. The Spanish founded the first lasting European settlement in what became the United States. This colony was begun at St. Augustine, Florida, in 1565. The Spanish also had settlements in the Southwest. The Dutch founded New Netherland in 1624. It later became New York. New Sweden was founded, in 1638, in what is now Delaware. The French founded Louisiana in 1699.

St. Augustine was the first lasting colony in the present-day United States. It was settled 42 years before Jamestown.

16. Are we having fun yet?

Most families lived in small houses. Families cooked, ate, and slept in one main room. Fathers and mothers worked. Children began working when they were about seven years old. Often they were sent to another family then.

This man in Jamestown made his living as a potter. A potter makes pottery, such as bowls, plates, and cups.

17. Will you bring me another cup of tea?

Rich families often had **indentured servants** and **slaves**. Most slaves were Africans. Some were Native Americans.

18. Did you hear about Betty Parris?

In 1692, in Salem, Massachusetts, nine-year-old Betty Parris began having fits. Soon other girls did, too. They claimed witches were hurting them. Nineteen people were hanged as witches. Many others were locked up, and six died. Then it turned out that Betty and her friends were just pretending.

The Salem Witch Trials took place in 1692. It is believed that up to 200 people were put in jail due to the witch hunt brought on by Betty Parris and the other girls.

19. Is it true we are not colonies anymore?

The Colonial period lasted about 170 years. It ended July 4, 1776, when the colonies said they were no longer England's colonies. They were a country called the United States of America.

20. Did you hear what Patrick Henry said?

The colonists had become very unhappy with the way England ruled them. They were angry about the taxes they had to pay. A leader in Virginia named Patrick Henry gave speeches that fired up the colonists. In 1775, he gave a speech that ended with these famous words: "Give me **liberty**, or give me death!" War soon followed. When it ended, the United States was a free country.

Glossary

colonies (KAH-luh-neez) New places where people move that are still ruled by the leaders of the country from which they came.

colonists (KAH-luh-nists) People who live in a colony.

compact (KOM-pakt) An agreement between two or more people or groups.

harvest (HAR-vist) A season's gathered crop.

indentured servants (in-DEN-churd SER-vints) People who have worked for another person for a fixed amount of time for payment of travel or living costs.

liberty (LIH-ber-tee) The state of being free.

religion (rih-LIH-jen) A belief in and a way of honoring a god or gods.

slaves (SLAYVZ) People who are "owned" by another person and forced to work for him or her.

turnips (TUR-neps) Plants with a thick root that can be eaten.

Index

Web Sites

Due to the changing nature of Internet links, PowerKids Press
has developed an online list of Web sites related to the subject of
this book. This site is updated regularly. Please use this link to
access the list:
www.powerkidslinks.com/20his/colam/

24